Springboards for Reading

38 Strategic Reading Lessons

Grades 7-12

by

Lori Mammen

ECS TestSMART™ Basic Skill-Building Lessons Software with Management System, Grades 1-10

Quality, cost-effective, sequential skill-builders for learners of all ability levels

	Number of Lessons	License for 1-5 CPUs	License for 6-15 CPUs	License for 16-24 CPUs	License for 25-up CPUs
Level 1-6 Reading	324	ECS2185-05	ECS2185-15	ECS2185-24	ECS2185
Level 1 Reading	54	ECS2045-05	ECS2045-15	ECS2045-24	ECS2045
Level 2 Reading	51	ECS2061-05	ECS2061-15	ECS2061-24	ECS2061
Level 3 Reading	54	ECS2088-05	ECS2088-15	ECS2088-24	ECS2088
Level 4 Reading	60	ECS210X-05	ECS210X-15	ECS210X-24	ECS210X
Level 5 Reading	58	ECS2126-05	ECS2126-15	ECS2126-24	ECS2126
Level 6 Reading	47	ECS2142-05	ECS2142-15	ECS2142-24	ECS2142
Level 7-10 Reading	81	ECS2169-05	ECS2169-15	ECS2169-24	ECS2169
Level 1-6 Math	172	ECS2193-05	ECS2193-15	ECS2193-24	ECS2193
Level 1 Math	17	ECS2053-05	ECS2053-15	ECS2053-24	ECS2053
Level 2 Math	33	ECS207X-05	ECS207X-15	ECS207X-24	ECS207X
Level 3 Math	24	ECS2096-05	ECS2096-15	ECS2096-24	ECS2096
Level 4 Math	35	ECS2118-05	ECS2118-15	ECS2118-24	ECS2118
Level 5 Math	24	ECS2134-05	ECS2134-15	ECS2134-24	ECS2134
Level 6 Math	39	ECS2150-05	ECS2150-15	ECS2150-24	ECS2150
Level 7-10 Math	68	ECS2177-05	ECS2177-15	ECS2177-24	ECS2177
Level 1-6 Reading & Math	496	ECS2207-05	ECS2207-15	ECS2207-24	ECS2207
Level 7-10 Reading & Math	149	ECS2215-05	ECS2215-15	ECS2215-24	ECS2215
All Levels Reading & Math	645	ECS2223-05	ECS2223-15	ECS2223-24	ECS2223

TestSMART™ Interactive Lessons, Grades 1-10

Great resource for improving test scores. Lessons cover all the IRA and NCTE standards.

	Number of Lessons	License for 1-10 CPUs	License for 11-24 CPUs	License for 25-up CPUs
Level 1-10 Reading/Lang. Arts	1145	ECSIL-10	ECSIL-24	ECSIL
Level 1 Reading/Lang. Arts	140	ECSIL1-10	ECSIL1-24	ECSIL1
Level 2 Reading/Lang. Arts	170	ECSIL2-10	ECSIL2-24	ECSIL2
Level 3 Reading/Lang. Arts	190	ECSIL3-10	ECSIL3-24	ECSIL3
Level 4 Reading/Lang. Arts	170	ECSIL4-10	ECSIL4-24	ECSIL4
Level 5 Reading/Lang. Arts	145	ECSIL5-10	ECSIL5-24	ECSIL5
Level 6 Reading/Lang. Arts	160	ECSIL6-10	ECSIL6-24	ECSIL6
Level 7-10 Reading/Lang. Arts	170	ECSIL7-10	ECSIL7-24	ECSIL7

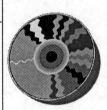

To order, visit www.educyberstor.com, or contact ECS Learning Systems, P.O. Box 791439, San Antonio, TX 78279.

Editor: Jennifer Knoblock
Page Layout & Graphics: Kathryn Riches
Cover/Book Design: Educational Media Services

ISBN 0-944459-70-6

Printed in the United States of America.

Table of Contents

Introduction   5
Objectives   6

Vocabulary   7
    Multiple Identities   9
    Sructural Analysis   10
    The "But" Game   11
    Jabberwocky   12
    Technical Diagrams   13
    What's My Line?   14

Facts and Details   15
    The 5-W Hunt   17
    Pertinent Information   18
    Step by Step   19
    Before and After   20
    Where's Home Base?   21
    Direction Derby   22

Main Idea   23
    Clip a Headline   25
    Looking for the Main Idea   26
    Western Union   27
    The Moral of the Story   28
    Summary Revision   29
    Summing Up   30

Causal Relationships   31
    Cause and Effect Chart   33
    Reading the Headlines   34
    Movie Mysteries   35
    The Person Most Likely To…   36

Inferences   37
    Graph the News   39
    Graphically Speaking   40
    Outer Space Conclusions   41
    Reading Between the Lines   42
    Generalizations   43
    Be More Specific   44
    Buy Me   45
    Understanding Characters   46
    Map a Story   47
    How Do You Feel About It?   48

Fact and Nonfact   49
    What's the Purpose?   51
    Point of View   52
    Convince Me   53
    To Find the Truth   54
    Just the Facts, Please   55
    Graphic Comparisons   56

Handouts   57
About the Author   78

Introduction

The lessons in this book serve as springboards for developing students' strategic reading skills and focus on six important areas of understanding and skill. These areas include vocabulary, facts and details, main idea, causal relationships, inferences, and fact/nonfact.

Each lesson addresses a particular reading skill in a "non-textbook" manner and emphasizes active student involvement through reading, discussion, cooperative learning activities, composition, creative and critical thinking, and other motivating activities. As students participate in the varied activities, they learn to monitor and adjust their reading for different purposes and different types of writing. By actively participating in the reading process, students develop the strategic reading skills they will need to be lifelong readers and learners.

Each lesson follows the same, easy-to-use format that includes the objective, materials/handouts, learning activities, and extension ideas for the lesson. While the lessons are grouped according to the skill they address, each lesson can be used independently. Therefore, teachers are free to select any lesson that is appropriate to their students' needs and interests.

Objectives

Vocabulary
- Use context clues to determine the meanings of multiple meaning words
- Use knowledge of prefixes and suffixes to determine word meanings
- Use context clues to determine meanings of unfamiliar words
- Use context clues to determine meanings of specialized/technical terms

Facts and Details
- Identify related details
- Arrange events in sequential order
- Follow complex written directions

Main Idea
- Identify the stated or paraphrased main idea of a selection
- Identify the implied main idea of a selection
- Identify the best summary of a selection

Causal Relationships
- Identify cause and effect relationships
- Predict probable future actions and outcomes

Inferences
- Interpret diagrams, graphs, and statistical illustrations
- Make inferences and draw conclusions
- Arrive at a generalization from a given series of details and/or assumptions
- Evaluate and make judgments
- Identify plot, setting, characters, and mood in literary selections

Fact and Nonfact
- Recognize author's point of view and purpose
- Recognize forms of propaganda and persuasive language
- Distinguish between fact and fiction
- Compare and contrast points of view on the same topic

Vocabulary

- Use context clues to determine the meanings of multiple meaning words

- Use knowledge of prefixes and suffixes to determine word meanings

- Use context clues to determine meanings of unfamiliar words

- Use context clues to determine meanings of specialized/technical terms

Multiple Identities

Lesson Objective

Students will use context clues to determine the meanings of multiple meaning words.

Materials/Handouts

Worksheet listing words with multiple meanings
Handout 1

Learning Activities

Begin by discussing multiple meaning words. Ask a student to name a word that has more than one meaning. Write the response on the chalkboard. Have students give at least three meanings the word could have. Challenge students to write a sentence for each of the word's meanings. Discuss how the other words in each sentence helped clarify the meaning of the multiple-meaning word. Note that these words are called context clues.

Provide several multiple meaning words for the students. Have students list three meanings for each word and write a sentence for each of the meanings. Once again, follow up with a discussion of context clues.

Note: Students should work with words related to their class work whenever possible.

Extensions

Give students a reading selection that includes several words with multiple meanings. Have them identify each multiple meaning word and give its definition as it is used in the passage. Discuss the context clues that helped students determine the word's meaning.

Structural Analysis

Lesson Objective

Students will use knowledge of prefixes and suffixes to determine word meanings.

Materials/Handouts

No special materials required
Handout 2

Learning Activities

Select vocabulary words from the content area/subject matter that the students are studying. The vocabulary words should have prefixes and/or suffixes.

Examples:
        substandard, circumspect, autocrat, bilateral, uniform

Ask students to pronounce each word. Discuss the possible meaning of each word. Ask the students if any parts of the words look familiar. Underline these parts of the words. Ask the students if they have seen or studied other words that have the same parts. List these words on the chalkboard.

Discuss with the students how prefixes/suffixes can help them determine the meaning of an unfamiliar word. Have the students list several words that have prefixes/suffixes and their meanings. How do their meanings relate to the prefix/suffix?

Extensions

Have students write riddles based on words that have prefixes/suffixes. Students should challenge each other with their riddles.

Divide the class into small groups. Distribute newspapers to each group. Instruct the students to examine the newspapers for words that contain prefixes or suffixes. The recorder in each group should write the words as the group discovers them. (Set a time limit on this exercise.) Then instruct the students to write the words on the chalkboard in like groups (i.e. uniform, unity, universe). Evaluate the answers as a class.

The "But" Game

Lesson Objective

Students will use knowledge of prefixes and suffixes to determine word meanings.

Materials/Handouts

Thesaurus, dictionary

Learning Activities

Divide the class into four to six teams. Distribute a thesaurus to each team. The members of each team should create at least ten sentences that include a set of antonyms, but leave one antonym's place blank.

Example:
>   Miss Granger's class was heterogeneous, but Mr. Bendle's class was _____.

After the teams have written the sentences, the teams should exchange papers. Each team then tries to complete their opponent's sentences correctly. The team that obtains the most correct answers wins. Evaluate the answers as a class.

Extensions

Make a list of all the antonyms used by the students. The class (in teams) should try to find as many synonyms to these words as they can.

Jabberwocky

Lesson Objective

Students will use context clues to determine the meanings of unfamiliar words.

Materials/Handouts

Copies of Lewis Carroll's poem *Jabberwocky* (one per student)

Learning Activities

Distribute a copy of *Jabberwocky* to each student. Read and discuss the poem with the students. (Many students probably will be familiar with the poem from their childhood.) During the discussion ask students if they have a clear picture in mind after reading the poem. (Most students will have a definite picture that is inspired by the meaning they attach to the poem.) Ask how they were able to make sense of the poem since Carroll used so many nonsense words. Connect their responses to the idea of using context clues to determine the meaning of an unfamiliar word.

Have the students work individually to rewrite *Jabberwocky*. They are to replace each of the nonsense words with a "real" word.

Discuss several of the student versions of *Jabberwocky*. Have the students justify why they used certain words in their version of the poem.

Extensions

Have the students illustrate their versions of *Jabberwocky*. Then arrange for them to read their poems and show their illustrations to a group of elementary students.

Give each student a reading selection with several unfamiliar words. Have students replace each unfamiliar word with another word that has the same/similar meaning. Discuss and critique student responses. Give each student a reading selection (preferably from the subject matter/content area of the class) that has blanks in place of certain key words. Have the students determine what word could correctly complete each part of the passage. (Make sure that the omitted word's meaning can be determined from the context clues.) Discuss and critique student responses.

Technical Diagrams

 Lesson Objective

Students will use context clues to determine the meanings of specialized/technical terms.

 Materials/Handouts

A collection of scientific or technical journals (copy four to six appropriate articles), dictionaries

 Learning Activities

Divide the class into small groups. Distribute an article to each group. The members of each group are to read the article, analyze the vocabulary, and list the key words. The group then chooses the word that represents the most inclusive concept in the article. The group then chooses words classified under the superordinate word chosen first. The group diagrams the relationship of the words. A dictionary should be used to verify the answers. The class should compare and critique diagrams.

Example:

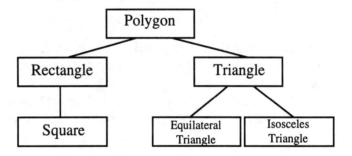

 Extensions

Each student summarizes the article using as many of the key vocabulary words as possible. Evaluate the summaries.

What's My Line?

 Lesson Objective

Students will use context clues to determine the meanings of specialized/technical terms.

 Materials/Handouts

Students will need access to several books on various careers. Work with the librarian to gather these materials and keep them on reserve for the students. Students will also need a supply of index cards.

 Learning Activities

Print the name of a different profession on index cards or slips of paper (one per student). Have each student select a card or paper and make note of the listed profession. Students should not tell others which profession they selected.

Tell the students their job is to research and discover several specialized/technical terms or vocabulary words that a person in the selected profession would know or use. The students should list these words on paper. Provide time for the students to research and find the information.

After the students have completed their research and listed the words, have them challenge other classmates to listen to the word list and guess the related profession.

Note: This strategy can be repeated with different topics. Examples could include rooms in a house, branches of science, school subjects, types of animals.

 Extensions

Have students create posters for their profession. The posters should have appropriate pictures and the listed words as an overview of the profession. Display the posters on a "career wall."

Have students categorize the words on their lists.

Facts and Details

- Identify related details

- Arrange events in sequential order

- Follow complex written directions

The 5-W Hunt

 Lesson Objective

Students will identify related details.

 Materials/Handouts

Newspapers, collection of pictures from calendars
Handout 3

 Learning Activities

Distribute a news or sports story to each student. Each student is to read the article and then answer the who, what, when, where, and why questions for the article. The questions and answers should then be exchanged with another student.

After each student has received the 5-W's, (s)he should write a news item using the information. (Students should not read the original article until their own articles are written.) A comparison between the original news item and the one written by the student should be made. If there is a great disparity between the two articles, students should determine why.

 Extensions

Distribute a calendar picture to each student. Have students list details in the picture. The pictures are then hung on a bulletin board. Have students take turns reading the details they listed about their pictures. Class members should identify the picture being described.

Pertinent Information

Lesson Objective

Students will identify related details.

Materials/Handouts

Selected reading passage (nonfiction)—one copy for each student, fact-finding worksheet (optional)
Handout 4 and 5

Learning Activities

Discuss with students that the facts and details included in a text should be central to the purpose of the text. Facts and details should serve as supports for the main idea/focus of a selection. Facts and details that are not central to the text's purpose give extraneous information that can distract or confuse the reader.

Give each student a copy of the selected passage/reading. As they read the selections, they should underline facts/details included in the text. After reading the passage, the students should determine the purpose of the selection. The students should write the purpose of the passage on notebook paper or on the fact-finding worksheet.

Have the students make two columns on the paper and label one column "Necessary Information" and the other column "Extra Information." Then the students should reread the selection, note the underlined facts/details, and decide if the fact/detail is central to understanding the text's purpose. Discuss their results. If there is disagreement about where certain facts/details have been placed, encourage justification of their answers.

Note: Include passages with extraneous facts/details.

Extensions

Review the information students wrote in the "Extra Information" column. Discuss why a writer would include extraneous information in a selection. Can the students think of a situation in which the "Extra Information" they have listed might become "Necessary Information"?

Step by Step

 Lesson Objective

Students will arrange events in sequential order.

 Materials/Handouts

Paper and pencil

 Learning Activities

Each student prepares an oral report that contains directions on how to make or do something. As the student gives the oral report, the rest of the class should be listening for sequential clues within the report. The class then lists the steps they hear in the oral directions given by the student. Students can place their reports on the board for others to read. A class discussion should determine if any direction could be made clearer or if an important step was left out or misplaced.

 Extensions

Students prepare directions for a recipe (in step form). The steps are cut apart and placed in an envelope. Envelopes are exchanged between students. Each student tries to put the steps in the correct sequence. Select one completed paper. The class should be prepared to make that recipe the next day in class.

Before and After

Lesson Objective

Students will arrange events in sequential order.

Materials/Handouts

Selected narrative (story or directions)—one copy for each student, cards or slips of paper with events/steps from narrative printed on them (one event/step per card)

Learning Activities

Have the students read the story/directions silently. After all the students have read the selection, select an event/step from the middle of the selection and write it on the chalkboard. Ask students when this event/step occurred in the selection.

Shuffle the cards/papers and select one. Read the event/step printed on the card/paper. Ask students if this event/step happened before or after the event written on the board. Allow students to discuss and reach a consensus. After students have decided, place the card either in a "before stack" or an "after stack" as indicated by the students.

Continue with each event/step listed until the students have sorted all the cards/papers correctly. Then have students take the "before stack" and correctly sequence each of the events/steps that appear on those cards/papers. Do the same with the "after stack." When all the cards/papers have been sequenced, have students check their sequencing with the original narrative.

Extensions

Have the students read a narrative (story or directions) that has a major event/step omitted. After students have finished reading the selection, write the omitted event/step on the chalkboard. Ask students where this event/step would fit. Have the students discuss the various responses and come to a consensus. Check the students' answer with the correct, complete narrative.

Discuss: Could certain events/steps occur at different points in a narrative and still be logical?

©ECS Learning Systems, Inc., San Antonio, TX

Where's Home Base?

Lesson Objective

Students will follow complex written directions.

Materials/Handouts

Advertisements with a map (junk mail), or travel magazines, or inserts in road maps

Learning Activities

Distribute one map to each student. The student selects a certain place on the map to be "home base." The student then writes detailed directions on how to find the place. The students exchange directions. Each student then draws a map based on another student's directions. The original map and the student's drawing should be compared. As a pair, students should decide how to change the directions to make them easier to follow. Display the directions and maps in the room.

Extensions

Select an article that tells how to make or do something and read it. List the steps in the article. If it is a recipe, the student could make it at home and then bring the results to school. Discuss how the directions could be stated more clearly.

Direction Derby

Lesson Objective

Students will follow complex written directions.

Materials/Handouts

Written directions that explain a process/activity familiar to most students—one copy per student (For the most part, these directions should be written in simple, one-step sentences. Therefore, the teacher may need to rewrite a more complex set of directions for this activity.)

Learning Activities

Give each student a copy of the written directions. Tell them that these directions are presented in simple sentences, and the students' job will be to rewrite them in a more mature, complex manner. Have students read through the directions. Instruct them to make note of single steps/ procedures that seem to be related and that could be combined into longer, more complex sentences. They should mark these sentences as they read.

Note: If the students have not worked with sentence combining, the teacher will want to spend some time on this topic before attempting this strategy. Sentence combining strategies can contribute to better reading and writing skills.

After the students have read the directions and marked the sentences that could be combined, they should rewrite the directions, combining the simple sentences whenever appropriate. Then the teacher and students should share and discuss both versions. Which version is easier to read? Why? Which would be easier to follow? Why? Lead students to understand that in many cases, directions are not written in simple sentences. Instead, authors often combine related substeps because this method can assist readers in understanding and following directions.

Extensions

Have students select a set of directions written in complex sentences that combine two or more small substeps. Instruct students to rewrite the directions in simple, one-step sentences.

©ECS Learning Systems, Inc., San Antonio, TX

Main Idea

- Identify the stated or paraphrased main idea of a selection

- Identify the implied main idea of a selection

- Identify the best summary of a selection

Clip a Headline

Lesson Objective

Students will identify the stated or paraphrased main idea of a selection.

Materials/Handouts

Newspapers, scissors, copy machine

Learning Activities

Select at least one article per student. Cut the headline from the articles and place the headlines on a bulletin board. Distribute one article to each student. The student should read the article and then choose the headline that best matches the article. Have a class discussion about why the student chose his/her particular headline. Evaluate the accuracy of the student selections.

Extensions

Have each student write a fictitious news item with a headline, separate the headline from the body of the article, and exchange papers with another student. Each student reads the article, matches it with the best headline, and then discusses the validity of the headline and/or how to make the headline more accurate.

Looking for the Main Idea

 Lesson Objective

Students will identify the stated or paraphrased main idea of a selection.

 Materials/Handouts

Nonfiction reading selection (related to content/subject, if possible)—one copy per student; supporting detail chart (optional)—one copy per student
Handout 6

 Learning Activities

Before working with the students, select a reading passage, determine its main idea, and list the supporting details. This information will be used during class time. Tell the students that they will determine the main idea of a reading selection by studying supporting details presented in the passage. Write the general topic of the selection on the chalkboard (Example: birds). Ask students to name all the possible main ideas for this broad topic. List these and allow time for discussion.

Write one of the passage's supporting details below the broad topic. Based on this supporting detail, what do students think is the main idea of the passage? Are any of the main ideas on their list still possibilities? Do any of their main ideas seem to be eliminated? Allow time for class discussion. Write another of the passage's supporting details below the broad topic. Follow the same analysis and discussion procedure as in the previous step. Continue in this manner until all the supporting details are listed on the chalkboard. Then ask each student to write the main idea of the passage on paper. Distribute the reading selection and have students read it and verify their main idea. Critique and discuss their answers.

 Extensions

Have students choose a reading selection, list its supporting details, and challenge a classmate to determine the main idea of the selection.

 ©ECS Learning Systems, Inc., San Antonio, TX

Western Union

Lesson Objective

Students will identify the implied main idea of a selection.

Materials/Handouts

Paper, short nonfiction articles

Learning Activities

Distribute a different article to each student. Direct the students to write a telegram using only the essential information from the article. Since telegrams are expensive, the students may only use twenty-five words or less. The students will exchange articles and telegrams. The students should evaluate the telegrams for accuracy. (Each telegram should state the main idea of the article.) Students should help each other revise the telegrams before submitting them to the teacher.

Extensions

After reading a short article, the student writes a title for the selection. The title should reflect the main idea of the article.

The Moral of the Story

 Lesson Objective

Students will identify the implied main idea of a selection.

 Materials/Handouts

Copies of several different fables—one fable per student (fables should not include the morals)
Handout 7

 Learning Activities

Although most students read fables in elementary school, they probably will need to review this type of story (format, purpose, etc.). After this review, distribute a fable to each student in the class. Allow time for each student to read the fable. Then ask the students to complete the following sentence for their own fable:

> The moral of this story is...

Organize students into groups of three to four. Have them read their fables to the other group members. Group members should suggest possible morals. Then the student who has read the fable should share the moral that (s)he gave the story. The group discusses and critiques the student's moral and tries to reach a consensus about the real moral of the fable. Follow up with large group discussion about this learning activity.

 Extensions

Challenge students to write an original fable for the same moral. Have them share their fables with other class members.

©ECS Learning Systems, Inc., San Antonio, TX

Summary Revision

Lesson Objective

Students will identify the best summary of a selection.

Materials/Handouts

Summaries written by the teacher, articles from textbooks or journals

Learning Activities

Present three summaries to the class: One summary should be stilted and somewhat awkward; one summary should be poor in content and form; and the third summary should contain all the main points and flow smoothly. Have the class read all three summaries and rate each summary. Next, have students (working in pairs) read the same article. Each student composes his/her own summary. The pair then reads each other's summary. Each student should give positive feedback to his/her partner about the accuracy of the summary. The summaries should be revised before submitting them to the teacher.

Extensions

With prior permission from several students, the class (as a whole) should critique some of the summaries. The merits of each one should be discussed along with suggestions for improvement.

Summing Up

Lesson Objective

Students will identify the best summary of a selection.

Materials/Handouts

Reading selections (related to content/subject, if possible)—one per student; prepared summary of one reading selection—one per student
Handout 8

Learning Activities

Give each student a copy of one reading selection and allow time for the students to read the passage carefully. After the students have read the passage, distribute the prepared summary to them. Explain that the second passage is a summary of the first. Provide time for the students to read the summary.

When students have read the summary, discuss the differences between the full passage and the summary. In addition to the obvious difference in length, what other changes do they note? List these differences on the chalkboard. Lead the students to develop some general rules for writing summaries.

After students have discussed the rules for summarizing, distribute a different reading selection. Have students read the passage. After reading the passage, students should use the summarizing rules and write a summary of the passage.

Discuss and critique student summaries.

Extensions

Select a newspaper article that would interest students. Clip the headline from the article. Distribute copies of the article to the students. Have them use the summarizing rules to write a summary of the passage. Challenge students to "summarize the summary" by creating a headline for the article. Compare student headlines to the original headline for the article.

  ©ECS Learning Systems, Inc., San Antonio, TX

Causal Relationships

- Identify cause and effect relationships

- Predict probable future actions and outcomes

Cause and Effect Chart

Lesson Objective

Students will identify cause and effect relationships.

Materials/Handouts

Graphic organizer design, short stories or articles (one for each pair of students)
Handout 9

Learning Activities

Pair the students and give each pair the same short story to read. After reading the story, one student will list several causes in a graphic design. The partner then provides the effect of each cause. The two students then discuss the validity of the answers. If they concur, then the two students should agree on after-effects (if any). The teacher should then evaluate the papers and comment on the responses.

Extensions

Have the class, as a whole, read a novel and complete a cause and effect graphic organizer for the novel during a group discussion.

Reading the Headlines

Lesson Objective

Students will identify cause and effect relationships.

Materials/Handouts

Several newspaper articles on different topics—one for each student

Learning Activities

Before class, cut the headlines from the newspaper articles. Number the articles and headlines so they can be matched again later.

Distribute one headline to each student in the class and allow time for the students to read their headlines. Discuss the fact that headlines tend to give results or effects. Ask students to study their headlines. Do they seem to give a result or an effect of something? If so, direct students to list two to three possible causes for this result or effect.

Example: Headline — LOCAL SCHOOL STUDENTS BRING HOME TROPHY

        Possible causes: The students won first place in an athletic event.
                              The students participated in a fund-raising activity for
                              charity and raised the most money.

After students have listed two or three causes, give them the articles that match their headlines. Have them read the articles and determine whether they were able to match the actual cause of the event.

Extensions

Read the articles to the entire class instead of distributing them to the students. Challenge students to match their headlines to the correct articles after they are read.

©ECS Learning Systems, Inc., San Antonio, TX

Movie Mysteries

Lesson Objective

Students will predict probable future actions and outcomes.

Materials/Handouts

Newspapers, magazines

Learning Activities

Divide the class into groups. Give each group a newspaper containing movie advertisements. Each group chooses a movie that no one in the group has seen. The group reads the title and any information about the movie in the advertisement. Each student then predicts what might happen in the movie. The students read their predictions to their group. A vote should be taken on the group's favorite prediction.

Extensions

The group views the movie and then compares each student's prediction to the actual outcome of the movie. The teacher should be aware of the movie's appropriateness for this age group.

The Person Most Likely To...

Lesson Objective

Students will predict probable future actions and outcomes.

Materials/Handouts

Several (five to six) fictional passages—one for each small group of students

Learning Activities

Organize students into groups of three to four. Give each group one of the fictional passages. The group is to read and discuss the passage. As part of the discussion, they should identify the main character and discuss him/her. (What is this character like? What are his/her interests? What are his/her problems?)

After students have completed this portion of the activity, write the following sentence stem on the chalkboard:

> You can tell from this passage that (main character) is most likely to...

Instruct the students to complete the sentence stem by inserting the name of their passage's main character and an appropriate conclusion based upon what they learned about the character from reading the passage. Each student should complete this step *individually*. When each student has completed the sentence, the results are shared and discussed in the small groups. Students should discuss and critique each person's answer. Students should pay particular attention to the reasonableness of each writer's prediction. Discuss and critique the results in a large group, as well.

Extensions

After reading a longer, complete work of fiction, have students make a prediction for the major characters in the work. However, each prediction should omit the name of the character. List the main characters on the chalkboard. Have a student read one of his/her predictions. Challenge the class to match the prediction to the correct character. Discuss and critique predictions and responses.

©ECS Learning Systems, Inc., San Antonio, TX

Inferences

- Interpret diagrams, graphs, and statistical illustrations

- Make inferences and draw conclusions

- Arrive at a generalization from a given series of details and/or assumptions

- Evaluate and make judgments

- Identify plot, setting, characters, and mood in literary selections

Graph the News

Lesson Objective

Students will interpret diagrams, graphs, and statistical illustrations.

Materials/Handouts

Graph paper, protractor, ruler, large selection of news magazines

Learning Activities

Group the students into small groups. Give each group one news magazine. The group should skim the magazine and choose an article that interests them and that has some graphs, charts, or statistical data related to the article. The group then reads the article, looks at the graphic sources for information, and writes five questions that pertain to the article and graphic sources.

The groups then trade articles and questions. After the questions are answered, each group prepares an oral report on their article's topic.

Extensions

Students collect weather details over an extended period of time. The students then design their own system of collecting and recording details. Graphs or charts should be prepared for display in the class. A discussion of each project can be held during class.

Graphically Speaking

 Lesson Objective

Students will interpret charts, diagrams, and statistical illustrations.

 Materials/Handouts

Samples of various types of graphic aids
Handout 10

 Learning Activities

Discuss the following graphic aids with the students:

      tables, pictographs, bar graphs, line graphs, pie graphs, charts, diagrams

Make sure that students can identify each type of graphic aid and know the purpose of each one. Organize students into groups of three to four. Each group is to select a topic, gather information on the topic, and show their findings with three different graphic aids. They must select the graphic aids that best suit the kind of results they will have.

Note: Before students begin this work, they should have a clear understanding of the type of information that can be shown in graphic aids. In addition, they should develop a list of methods for gathering information (simple research, interviews, surveys, etc).

At the end of the project, students should present their information and graphic aids to the class.

Note: This project will take several class periods or require work outside class.

 Extensions

Have students prepare a school display of their graphics.

Have students develop questions that can be answered by studying the information presented in their graphic aids. Then have them challenge other teams to interpret the graphic aids and answer the questions.

©ECS Learning Systems, Inc., San Antonio, TX

Outer Space Conclusions

Lesson Objective

Students will make inferences and draw conclusions.

Materials/Handouts

Newspapers or magazines
Handout 11

Learning Activities

Divide the class into pairs. Each student is to choose pictures from newspapers or magazines that depict life on earth. After the pictures are collected, they are to be exchanged with the partner. Each partner is to pretend that (s)he is a visitor from another galaxy. Each student is to look at the pictures and write at least five conclusions about life on earth. The pictures should be displayed in the classroom, and the conclusions should be shared orally in class. Discussion should include how logical the conclusions were (based on the pictures as the only supporting data).

Extensions

Have students write a short article based on a group of pictures of their choice. Articles should be shared with other students.

Reading Between the Lines

Lesson Objective

Students will make inferences and draw conclusions.

Materials/Handouts

Several declarative statements
Handout 12

Learning Activities

Make sure that students understand the meaning of "inference" before proceeding with this lesson. (An inference is a conclusion based on a set of facts or ideas.)

Write a declarative statement on the chalkboard and ask the students to make an inference based upon the statement.

After the students have listed several inferences, discuss how they can determine if an inference is true or accurate. (There should be enough information to support the inference.)

Continue in the same manner with other declarative statements.

Extensions

Have students do a similar exercise with photographs. They should study a photograph and list two to three inferences they might make based on the information in the picture.

Generalizations

Lesson Objective

Students will arrive at a generalization from a given series of details and/or assumptions.

Materials/Handouts

Newspapers and magazines

Learning Activities

Divide the class into small groups. Give each group a stack of newspapers and/or magazines. Each group sorts through the periodicals and cuts out those articles that contain generalizations. Each group should write the generalizations on the chalkboard or large tablet. The generalizations can be exchanged and the group can rewrite any generalization that is not true.

Extensions

Each group should choose an article that contains generalizations that are not true and then rewrite the article with conclusions that are true.

Be More Specific

Lesson Objective

Students will arrive at a generalization from a given series of details and/or assumptions.

Materials/Handouts

Sets of specific statements on several topics
Handout 13

Learning Activities

Tell students they will be using specific statements to make a generalization on a variety of topics. Write the first set of specific statements on the chalkboard.

Example: Topic—The weather on a particular day

Specific statements—

1. The temperature was twenty-two degrees.
2. The wind was blowing forty-three miles per hour.
3. There were three inches of snow on the ground.

Ask students what generalization they could make based on these specifics. Discuss answers.

Possible generalization—Most people will want to stay inside today.

Continue with other sets of specific statements.

Extensions

Provide a generalization based on the subject matter/content in the textbook. Have students find four to five specific statements from the text that would support the generalization.

Buy Me

Lesson Objective

Students will evaluate and make judgments.

Materials/Handouts

Magazines, *Consumer Reports* magazine

Learning Activities

Give each student a magazine. Each student is to find an advertisement that promotes a product appealing to him/her. The student reads and records all the information about the product in the ad. The student then tries to find additional information about this product from other sources, (i.e. *Consumer Reports,* interviews with people who have bought the product, letters to companies for additional information). After all sources have been explored, the student then writes an essay on why the chosen product would or would not be a wise purchase.

Extensions

Oral reports can be given to the class. Discussions on the decision to buy or not to buy should be held.

Understanding Characters

Lesson Objective

Students will evaluate and make judgments.

Materials/Handouts

No special materials needed

Learning Activities

Each student selects a character from a novel/short story and writes a three to four sentence character summary for the character. Then the student refers to the story and finds specific actions, statements, or other evidence to prove that the character summary is accurate.

After all the students have written a summary and gathered evidence, have them work with partners. Each partner reads the specific actions, statements, or other evidence of the character's personality. The other partner listens and then completes the following sentence stem:

My partner has provided evidence that proves (character's name) is/was...

After the student has completed the sentence stem, (s)he compares the answer to the character summary written by the other partner. The partners should discuss any differences in their analysis of the chosen character. Both students should have a turn to read their evidence list and write an answer for the other partner's evidence.

Follow-up with a class discussion and critique of this activity.

Extensions

As a preview of an upcoming reading assignment, select a character from a novel/short story and give students a list of specific actions, statements, or other evidence of the character's personality. The students then complete the following sentence stem about the character.

From the evidence provided, it is clear that (character's name) is/was...

Discuss and critique student answers. Have students use the information gathered from this assignment to direct their reading of the novel/short story.

©ECS Learning Systems, Inc., San Antonio, TX

Map a Story

Lesson Objective

Students will identify plot, setting, characters, and mood in literary selections.

Materials/Handouts

Overhead projector, paper, pencils
Handout 14

Learning Activities

Have the students read a short story. After the story has been read, help the students generate a story map. Help the class develop the map by thinking out loud, asking questions, or explaining connections between events.

Extensions

Have students prepare a story map for an episode of a favorite television program.

How Do You Feel About It?

Lesson Objective

Students will identify plot, setting, characters, and mood in literary selections.

Materials/Handouts

Copies of various fictional selections—one per student

Learning Activities

Distribute a fictional selection to each student. Tell students to read the passage, determine the mood of the selection, and note it on their paper. Then they should reread the selection and make a list of words/phrases that help establish the mood of the piece.

When the students have completed this activity, discuss and critique the results.

Extensions

Distribute copies of student-written work and have the students use the same strategy as above. Students can use the results to help them in revision of their own writing.

Fact and Nonfact

- Recognize author's point of view and purpose

- Recognize forms of propaganda and persuasive language

- Distinguish between fact and nonfact

- Compare and contrast points of view on the same topic

What's the Purpose?

Lesson Objective

Students will recognize the author's point of view and purpose.

Materials/Handouts

Newspapers, magazines, scissors, glue, junk mail, catalogs, large envelopes

Learning Activities

Give each student four large envelopes. On the outside of each envelope write one of the following phrases:

> To persuade
> To give a biased viewpoint
> To give advice
> To give information

Have students look through the reading materials and find articles that depict each of the four purposes. The students cut out the articles and place them it in the corresponding envelope. Students exchange envelopes with each other. The students check each other's work for accuracy. Hold discussions if disagreements occur.

Extensions

Each student writes a short article for each of the four purposes. Students should share their work and give each other positive feedback.

Point of View

Lesson Objective

Students will recognize the author's point of view and purpose.

Materials/Handouts

Several news articles about the same event/topic, but from several different newspapers and/or magazines—one article for every two to three students
Handout 15

Learning Activities

Begin with a discussion of the event/topic that is the subject of the articles. Have students take notes on what they seem to know about the topic.

Organize students into groups and give each group one of the articles. The group is to read the article and answer the following questions when they are finished reading:

1. Is the author's view of the event/subject generally positive or negative?
2. How would you summarize the author's views on the event/subject? (2-3 sentences)
3. What words/phrases does the author use that give evidence of his/her feelings about the subject?

When each group has completed this phase of the activity, follow-up with a class discussion and critique of their responses. As part of the follow-up, have the students determine which authors' viewpoints seem to be most conflicting; determine which authors' viewpoints seem to be most similar; group the articles as follows—generally positive, generally negative, generally neutral; and sequence the articles from most negative to most positive.

Extensions

Each student can collect four to six articles on a current event/subject and complete this activity. Results can be presented on a chart or poster.

Convince Me

Lesson Objective

Students will recognize forms of propaganda and persuasive language.

Materials/Handouts

Scissors, glue, newspapers, magazines, junk mail, catalogs, construction paper

Learning Activities

Students look through the reading material that is available and find four advertisements that attempt to persuade or convince someone to buy or do something. The students cut out the advertisements or articles and glue them to a piece of construction paper. On the back, the students write which persuasive techniques were used in each advertisement. (Some persuasive techniques include: name calling, transfer, bandwagon, plain folks, glittering generalities, and card stacking.) Students then exchange advertisements and evaluate each other's answers.

After the review, assign students to work in small groups to create a collage for each of the propaganda techniques. Each group works on one technique. Distribute old magazines and newspapers. Students should find advertisements and/or articles that use the propaganda technique assigned to their group. These are clipped from the periodical and arranged on the poster board as a collage.

Follow-up with a class presentation and discussion of each group's collage.

Extensions

Each student should choose one persuasive technique and use it to write an original advertisement. The class should decide which technique was used.

To Find the Truth

Lesson Objective

Students will distinguish between fact and nonfact.

Materials/Handouts

Newspapers, magazines, scissors, envelopes, timer

Learning Activities

Divide the class into teams of three or four. Set the timer for ten minutes. Each team is to find as many factual headlines as they can. They should cut out the factual headlines and put them in an envelope. After the timer rings, groups should exchange envelopes. Each group is to evaluate the accuracy of the items in the envelope and then share the headlines with the whole class.

Extensions

The headlines in the envelopes can be rewritten as opinions, not facts. Have students share the results with the class.

 ©ECS Learning Systems, Inc., San Antonio, TX

Just the Facts, Please

Lesson Objective

Students will distinguish between fact and nonfact.

Materials/Handouts

Old magazines and newspapers

Learning Activities

Distribute old magazines and newspapers to the students. Instruct them to scan several magazines and newspapers and find examples of opinions. The opinions may be from headlines, advertisements, articles, or any other section of the periodical. The students find ten opinions and write them on paper. For each opinion, students should circle words that indicate that the statement is not a factual statement. Then they rewrite each of the ten opinions as facts.

As a follow-up, allow time for discussion and critique of student work.

Extensions

Have students use the same method to find ten factual statements from periodicals. They should circle words that indicate the statements are facts and then rewrite them as opinions.

Graphic Comparisons

 Lesson Objective

Students will compare and contrast points of view on the same topic.

 Materials/Handouts

Blackline master for comparisons, magazines, short stories, articles
Handout 16

 Learning Activities

Have a pair of students select an article to read. As they are reading, they jot down points for comparison and contrast. Students then complete the graphic organizer.

Some articles should be discussed in class. All graphics should be displayed in the classroom.

 Extensions

Have students exchange graphics with another pair of students and summarize the article by looking only at the completed graphic.

Handouts

This section includes the handouts referenced in the lessons.

Handout 1
Multiple Identities

alarm

band

book

brush

draw

grade

hand

iron

left

light

note

pack

pass

present

prime

race

rap

right

share

step

stock

track

trip

watch

Prefixes	Suffixes
anti-	-able
bi-	-al
co-	-ance
con-	-ar
de-	-ate
dis-	-dom
fore-	-ence
hemi-	-ent
in-	-er
inter-	-fy
mal-	-hood
multi-	-ing
non-	-ion
poly-	-ist
post-	-ize
pre-	-less
re-	-ly
semi-	-ment
super-	-ness
trans-	-or
tri-	-sion
un-	-tion
under-	
uni-	

Handout 3
The 5–W Hunt

Who? _____

What? _____

When? _____

Where? _____

Why? _____

News Story—

_____

_____

_____

_____

_____

_____

_____

_____

_____

_____

_____

©ECS Learning Systems, Inc., San Antonio, TX   61

Fact-finding Worksheet

Who? _____

What? _____

When? _____

Where? _____

Why? _____

This passage is mostly about

_____

_____

_____

_____

The main purpose of this passage is

_____

_____

_____

_____

©ECS Learning Systems, Inc., San Antonio, TX

Handout 5
Pertinent Information

This passage is mostly about _____.

Necessary information	Extra information

Handout 6
Looking for the Main Idea

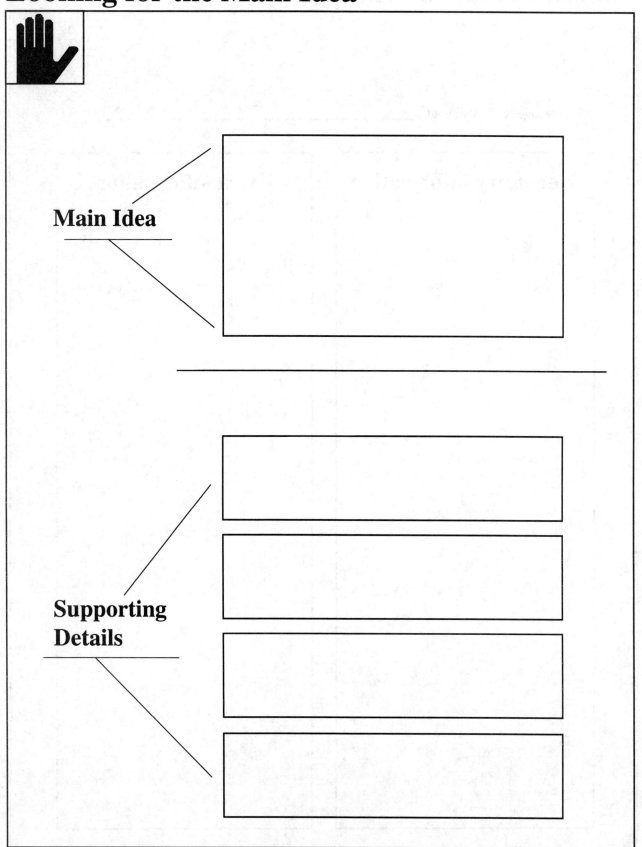

Main Idea

Supporting Details

©ECS Learning Systems, Inc., San Antonio, TX

Handout 7
The Moral of the Story

Morals

Beware of a wolf in sheep's clothing.

Don't count your chickens before they hatch.

Slow and steady wins the race.

Patience is a virtue.

A watched pot never boils.

A hero must have brave deeds as well as brave words.

Th end of a story depends on who tells it.

Misery loves company.

1. Remove information that does not contribute to the passage's main purpose.

2. Remove information that simply repeats something that has already been stated in the passage.

3. Look for the topic sentence of each paragraph and circle it. The topic sentence usually is a summary of the paragraph.

4. Create a topic sentence for any paragraph that does not have one.

5. Replace lists of words, actions, or phrases with a more inclusive term whenever possible. (Example: Instead of saying "my brother, sister, mother, and father," say "my family.")

Handout 9
Cause and Effect Chart

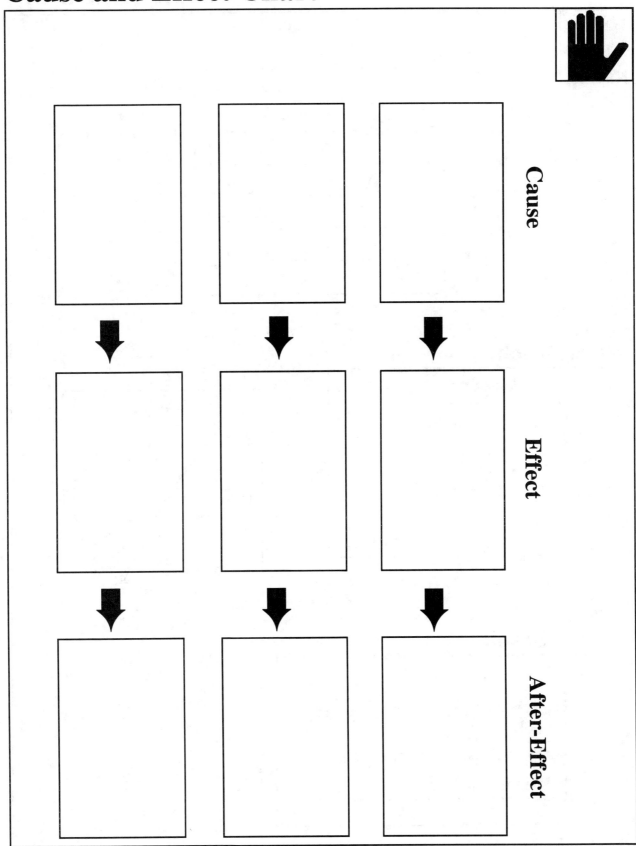

Line Graph

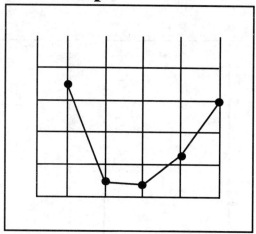

Pictograph

Feeding the Dog

Mark   " " " " "

Sarah   " "

Chris   " " "

Suzi   "

" = 1 Day

Pie Chart

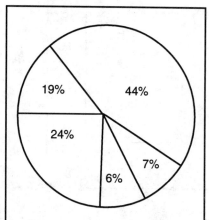

Bar Graph

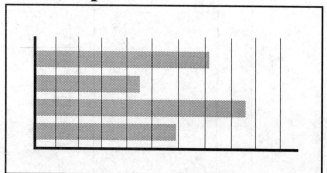

©ECS Learning Systems, Inc., San Antonio, TX

Handout 11
Outer Space Conclusions

Attach picture(s) here.

Conclusions about life on earth:

_____

_____

_____

_____

_____

_____

_____

_____

_____

Maria walked to school this morning.

1.

2.

3.

David wore a suit and tie when he went to school.

1.

2.

3.

Mr. and Mrs. Edison want to purchase a new and larger car.

1.

2.

3.

The delivery truck made several stops on Madison Boulevard.

1.

2.

3.

 ©ECS Learning Systems, Inc., San Antonio, TX

Handout 13
Be More Specific

Specific Statements

The temperature was twenty-two degrees.
The wind was blowing forty-three miles per hour.
There were three inches of snow on the ground.

Possible Generalization

_____

_____

Specific Statements

Audrey was the president of her class.
Audrey played on the basketball and soccer teams.
Audrey was a volunteer at the county hospital three days a week.

Possible Generalization

_____

_____

Specific Statements

Timothy arrived late for basketball practice three times last week.
Timothy forgot to submit his book report in English class.
Timothy did not do the chores assigned to him at home.

Possible Generalization

_____

_____

Handout 14
Map a Story

Characters ______________________ ______________________

______________________ ______________________

______________________ ______________________

Setting ____

Problem ____

Event **1.** ______________________________

2. ______________________________

3. ______________________________

Solution ____

Mood ____

Handout 15
Point of View

1. Is the author's view of the event/subject generally positive or negative?

2. How would you summarize the author's views on the event/subject?
    (2-3 sentences)

3. What words/phrases does the author use that give evidence of his/her feelings about the subject?

1. Which authors' viewpoints seem to be most conflicting?

2. Which authors' viewpoints seem to be most similar?

3. Group the articles as follows—generally positive, generally negative, generally neutral.

4. Sequence the articles as follows—from most negative to most positive.

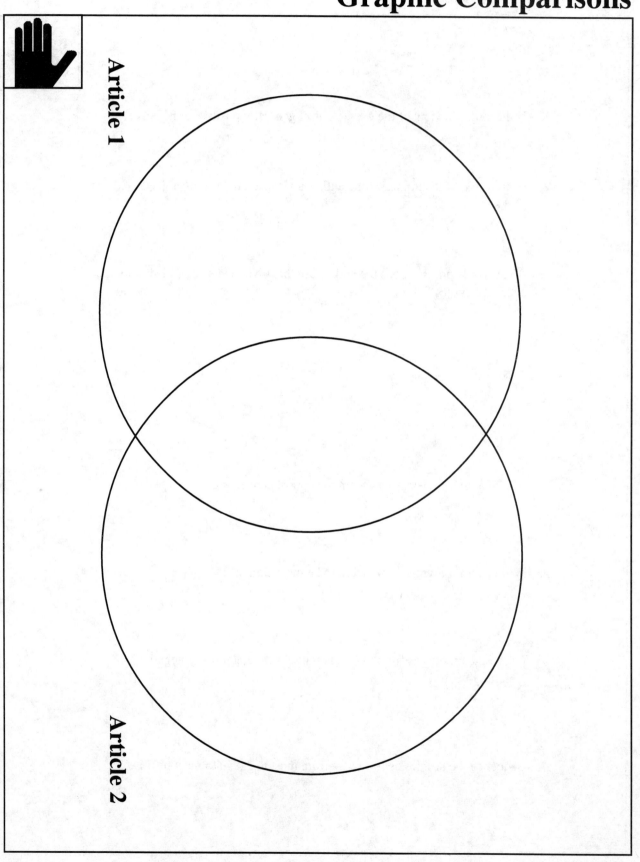

Article 1

Article 2

Notes

the magazine for reading · writing · thinking

Essential Reading for the Busy Classroom Professional

Benefit from this timely magazine for teachers, third grade through young adult. The new r•w•t™ magazine combines two award-winning publications—*Writing Teacher*™ and *THINK*™—for today's changing world.

Each issue contains—

- lively, informative articles on reading, writing, and thinking;
- hands-on ideas for today's grades 3-8 classrooms;
- 12-16 reproducible pages of challenging, ready-to-use activities;
- in-depth interviews with leading authors and educators;
- columns on special topics, including critical issues in reading, writing, and thinking;
- and success stories shared by educators like yourself.

> "I just received the new r•w•t™ today, and it looks great! ...I appreciate your magazine and its great ideas." —Kentucky

30%–off Special Offer!
Save $7.50.
Order r•w•t™ magazine with your book order for only $17.50 per year.

A world of ideas for a full year—

September 2001	Our Day-to-Day World Reading, Writing, and Thinking About What Everyone Needs to Know
November 2001	What Was It Like When *You* Were Growing Up? Reading, Writing, and Thinking Across the Generations
January 2002	Giggles in the Classroom Reading, Writing, and Thinking with Humor and Wit
March 2002	Saving the Earth for Our Grandchildren's Grandchildren Reading, Writing, and Thinking About the Environment
May 2002	Thinking Beyond Tests Reading, Writing, and Thinking in the Age of Standardized Assessment

Lesson Plans • Calendar Activities • Idea Exchange
for Reading • Writing • Thinking

☐ **Yes!** I want to subscribe to r•w•t.

Please enter my r•w•t subscription for: (please check one)

☐ 1 Year $25   ☐ 2 Years $45   ☐ 3 Years $65

☐ **Yes! I want to save 30%.** I have placed a book order of $400 or more. See coupon on page 54 for details.

Please enter my r•w•t subscription for: (please check one)

☐ 1 Year $17.50   ☐ 2 Years $31.50   ☐ 3 Years $45.50

Mail to: r•w•t™
P.O. Box 791439
San Antonio, TX 78279

e-mail:
rwtmagazine@
educyberstor.com

All non-U.S. subscriptions, please add $6.00 postage and handling in U.S. funds. Please allow 8–10 weeks for delivery of your first issue.

_____
Name of the individual (not the school)

_____
Mailing address

_____
City   State   Zip

(_____)_____
Daytime Telephone number

Personal subscriptions must be prepaid.

Complete Items Below:

☐ Check/M.O. Enclosed

☐ Charge to: ___VISA___MC___AmEX___Discover

Card No: _____ Exp. _____

Cardholder's Name: _____

Signature: _____

About the Author

Lori Mammen, a professional educator for 20 years, is a graduate of The Ohio State University in Columbus, Ohio. She is the co-creator and editor of *Writing Teacher*™ and *THINK*™ magazines, and works with teachers in the areas of composition, reading, and thinking skills.

Lori lives with her husband Sam and children Sarah, Suzanne, and Christopher in Bulverde, Texas.

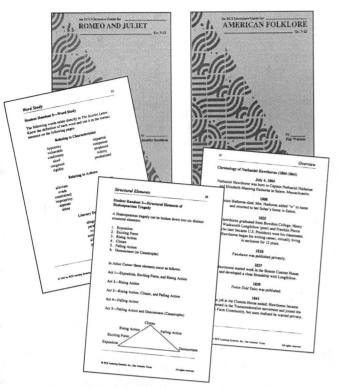

Literature Guides

Everything you need to teach a novel, right at your fingertips

These value-priced, 6" X 9" compact-sized guides for some of today's most popular novels help teachers develop a strong literature program.

- Reproducible student activity sheets, overhead transparency masters, and tests save valuable preparation time.

- Background information and teaching strategies are especially helpful for a teacher new to the literature selection.

- The guides include writing assignments and extension activities that encourage higher-ordered thinking.

ECS1294	Easy Order Set of All 17 Books		$186.15
ECS9560	American Folklore	96pp.	
ECS0441	Beowulf/The Hobbit	128pp.	
ECS9544	The Canterbury Tales	80pp.	
ECS059X	The Crucible	112pp.	
ECS9994	Great Expectations	96pp.	
ECS0093	Hamlet	96pp.	
ECS1006	Julius Caesar	80pp.	
ECS9951	Lord of the Flies	96pp.	
ECS9978	Macbeth	96pp.	
ECS0050	Mayor of Casterbridge/ Far from Madding Crowd	112pp.	
ECS0468	The Miracle Worker	96pp.	
ECS9579	The Return of the Native	96pp.	
ECS9897	Romeo and Juliet	80pp.	
ECS0042	The Scarlet Letter	96pp.	
ECS965X	A Tale of Two Cities	96pp.	
ECS9536	To Kill a Mockingbird	96pp.	
ECS9552	Wuthering Heights	96pp.	

Value-priced for only $10.95 each

Time-Savers

- Each guide includes the following: background information about the author, overview of the literature selection, vocabulary lists, teaching strategies, research and creative writing assignments, objective and essay tests, and extension activities.
- Ideal for grades 7-12!

Inkblots
A Guide for Creative Writing
by Pat Watson and Janet Watson

Comprehensive, organized lessons for teaching emergent writers how to brainstorm, keep journals, collaborate, write independently, and much more.

You want your students to succeed at creative writing but don't always have time to develop the lesson plans you need. From understanding writing stages to word studies, *Inkblots* books address all the fundamentals for teaching creative writing. Each guide provides easy-to-use lesson plans, complete with grade-appropriate activities and assignments that help young minds reach their creative potential. Fun and well-developed lessons give students the kind of practice they need to become successful writers.

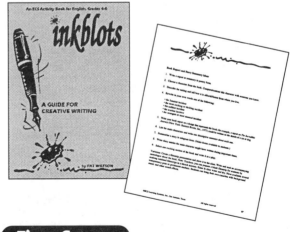

ECS2738	Easy Order Set of All 3 Books			$44.85
ECS1790	Inkblots	112pp.	Gr. K-3	$14.95
ECS1804	Inkblots	128pp.	Gr. 4-6	$15.95
ECS9609	Inkblots	96pp.	Gr. 6-12	$13.95

Time-Savers

- Each guide includes the following sections: Getting Started, Journaling, Letter Writing, Developing a Writing Program, Writing Assignments, A Closer Look at Stories, A Closer Look at Poetry, Reading and Writing Connection, Short Assignments, Student Handouts, and Student Work.
- *Inkblots K-3* provides additional activities for group stories, dictated stories, picture stories, and story writing.
- *Inkblots 4-6* contains a creative research section.

Novel Units® Literature Guides

When you're serious about having a quality reading/literature program℠

Find refreshing new ways to teach reading, writing, thinking, and the love of literature. These easy-to-use, complete guides have everything needed to teach a book.

Two components, a Teacher Guide and a Student Packet, provide a comprehensive teaching unit, however each guide can be successfully used alone. Teacher Guides average 32+ pages, and reproducible Student Packets average 44+ pages.

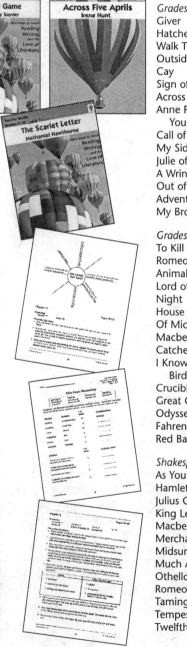

Grades 1-2	Teacher Guide $9.95
Frog and Toad (3 books)	NU2072
Amelia Bedelia	NU0231
Miss Nelson (2 books)	NU0320
Corduroy (2 books)	NU0045
Nate the Great and the Sticky Case	NU2633
Polar Express	NU1963
Ox-Cart Man	NU4571
Where the Wild Things Are	NU0223
Strega Nona	NU279X
Madeline's Rescue	NU4733
One Fine Day	NU2498
Stone Soup	NU2013
Sylvester and the Magic Pebble	NU0193
Why Mosquitoes Buzz in People's Ears	NU4784

Grades 3-4	Teacher Guide $9.95	Student Packet $11.95
Stone Fox	NU0630	NU6337SP
Sarah, Plain and Tall	NU2471	NU6329SP
Charlotte's Web	NU0266	NU6302SP
Whipping Boy	NU0894	NU7112SP
Freckle Juice	NU0088	NU8224SP
James and the Giant Peach	NU055X	NU4873SP
Lion, the Witch, and the Wardrobe	NU2439	NU704XSP
Sadako and the Thousand Paper Cranes	NU1785	NU6310SP
Chocolate Touch	NU0479	NU8259SP
Ramona Quimby, Age 8	NU4482	NU7082SP
Charlie & the Chocolate Factory	NU1904	NU7023SP
Snow Treasure	NU2854	
Tales of a Fourth Grade Nothing	NU2714	NU7090SP
Best Christmas Pageant Ever	NU1971	NU7015SP
Cricket in Times Square	NU3966	NU8356SP

Grades 5-6		
Number the Stars	NU2544	NU6051SP
Island of the Blue Dolphins	NU2528	NU489XSP
Bridge to Terabithia	NU248X	NU4881SP
Maniac Magee	NU3486	NU6043SP
Shiloh	NU4245	NU606XSP
Tuck Everlasting	NU251X	NU4903SP
Egypt Game	NU5004	NU8240SP
Dear Mr. Henshaw	NU2579	NU7139SP
From the Mixed-Up Files of Mrs. Basil E. Frankweiler	NU2269	NU7147SP
True Confessions of Charlotte Doyle	NU4792	NU8291SP
Roll of Thunder, Hear My Cry	NU0851	NU525XSP
Catherine, Called Birdy	NU7929	NU7937SP
How to Eat Fried Worms	NU2048	NU7155SP
Bunnicula	NU2005	NU7120SP
Pinballs	NU0827	NU8275SP

Grades 7-8	Teacher Guide $9.95	Student Packet $11.95
Giver	NU6183	NU7171SP
Hatchet	NU1238	NU4938SP
Walk Two Moons	NU7708	NU7716SP
Outsiders	NU3621	NU4067SP
Cay	NU3141	NU4121SP
Sign of the Beaver	NU2420	NU4954SP
Across Five Aprils	NU0916	NU4911SP
Anne Frank: The Diary of a Young Girl	NU0983	NU6078SP
Call of the Wild	NU1386	NU5292SP
My Side of the Mountain	NU1068	NU4946SP
Julie of the Wolves	NU1025	NU8216SP
A Wrinkle in Time	NU1181	NU4989SP
Out of the Dust	NU5893	NU5907SP
Adventures of Tom Sawyer	NU3567	NU5284SP
My Brother Sam Is Dead	NU380X	NU8232SP

Grades 9-12		
To Kill a Mockingbird	NU1572	NU3079SP
Romeo and Juliet	NU3745	NU3753SP
Animal Farm	NU3052	NU3060SP
Lord of the Flies	NU3834	NU3842SP
Night	NU8046	NU8054SP
House on Mango Street	NU4830	NU5591SP
Of Mice and Men	NU1874	NU3109SP
Macbeth	NU4369	NU4377SP
Catcher in the Rye	NU4490	NU4504SP
I Know Why the Caged Bird Sings	NU4849	NU6345SP
Crucible	NU363X	NU3648SP
Great Gatsby	NU3168	NU3176SP
Odyssey	NU7600	NU7619SP
Fahrenheit 451	NU301X	NU3028SP
Red Badge of Courage	NU346X	NU3478SP

Shakespeare Titles		
As You Like It	NU5047	NU5055SP
Hamlet	NU4180	NU4199SP
Julius Caesar	NU3036	NU3044SP
King Lear	NU9239	NU9247SP
Macbeth	NU4369	NU4377SP
Merchant of Venice	NU5664	NU5672SP
Midsummer Night's Dream	NU5187	NU5195SP
Much Ado About Nothing	NU9255	NU9263SP
Othello	NU5209	NU5217SP
Romeo and Juliet	NU3745	NU3753SP
Taming of the Shrew	NU7686	NU7694SP
Tempest	NU6272	NU6280SP
Twelfth Night	NU5869	NU5877SP

For a complete catalog, call 1-800-688-3224.